The Jewish Victims of the Holocaust

–The Holocaust in History–

The Jewish Victims of the Holocaust

Linda Jacobs Altman

Enslow Publishers, Inc.

40 Industrial Road   PO Box 38
Box 398   Aldershot
Berkeley Heights, NJ 07922   Hants GU12 6BP
USA   UK
http://www.enslow.com

Library of Congress Cataloging-in-Publication Data

Altman, Linda Jacobs, 1943-
    The Jewish victims of the Holocaust / Linda Jacobs Altman.
        v. cm. — (The Holocaust in history)
    Includes index.
    Contents: A people dispossessed — The ghettos of Eastern Europe —
Organizing murder — Living and dying in the camps — Marching to nowhere.
    ISBN 0-7660-1992-6
    1. Holocaust, Jewish (1939-1945)—Juvenile literature. 2. Germany—
History—1933-1945—Juvenile literature. [1. Holocaust, Jewish (1939-1945)
2. Germany—History—1933-1945.] I. Title. II. Series.
D804.34 A495 2003
940.53'18—dc21

                                                                        2002151084

Printed in the United States of America

10 9 8 7 6 5 4 3 2 1

To Our Readers: We have done our best to make sure all Internet Addresses in this
book were active and appropriate when we went to press. However, the author and
the publisher have no control over and assume no liability for the material avail-
able on those Internet sites or on other Web sites they may link to. Any comments
or suggestions can be sent by e-mail to comments@enslow.com or to the address
on the back cover.

Illustration Credits: Archiwum Akt Nowych (former Communist Party Archives),
courtesy of USHMM Photo Archives, pp. 32, 54; Archiwum Dokumentocj
Mechanizney, courtesy of USHMM Photo Archives, p. 10; Belarussian State
Archive of Documentary Film and Photography, courtesy of USHMM Photo
Archives, p. 84; courtesy of Jillian Saridaki, pp. 59, 61; courtesy of the Simon
Wiesenthal Center, p. 57; courtesy of USHMM Photo Archives, pp. 2, 3, 5, 12, 11,
16, 21, 22, 31, 34, 36, 38, 49, 56, 68, 71 (both), 77; Emanuel Hersch, courtesy of
USHMM Photo Archives, p. 41; Enslow Publishers, Inc., pp. 9, 58; Harry S. Truman
Library, courtesy of USHMM Photo Archives, p. 52; James Sanders, courtesy of
USHMM Photo Archives, p. 6; KZ Gedenkstatte Dachau, courtesy of USHMM
Photo Archives, pp. 47, 75, 83; Library of Congress, pp. 27, 74, 79; Library of
Congress, courtesy of USHMM Photo Archives, p. 18; Main Commission for the
Investigation of Nazi War Crimes, courtesy of USHMM Photo Archives, pp. 1, 29,
42, 45, 48, 64; National Archives, pp. 26, 44, 81, 86; National Archives, courtesy of
USHMM Photo Archives, pp. 63, 66, 88; National Museum in Majdanek, courtesy
of USHMM Photo Archives, p. 73; Rafal Imbro, courtesy of USHMM Photo
Archives, p. 35; Sabina Weinstock Goldstein, courtesy of USHMM Photo Archives,
p. 28; Stadtarchiv Mittweida, courtesy of USHMM Photo Archives, p. 19; State
Archives of the Russian Federation, courtesy of USHMM Photo Archives, p. 14.

Cover Illustration: Courtesy of USHMM Photo Archives

Contents

Under the rule of Adolf Hitler, German troops invaded
Poland on September 1, 1939, beginning World War II.

Introduction
World War II and the Holocaust

On September 1, 1939, German troops invaded Poland. Two days later, Britain and France declared war on Germany. World War II had begun. Under Adolf Hitler and his National Socialist German Workers' Party, also called the Nazi party, Germany would soon conquer most of Europe.

Hitler planned to build a *Reich*, or empire, that would last for a thousand years. He believed that Northern Europeans, or Aryans as he called them, were a master race—a group of people superior to others.

Hitler falsely believed that some people were inferior, such as Jews, Gypsies, Poles, Russians, and people of color. These people would be given no rights in his Reich. Some would be exterminated, or killed. Others would be kept alive only so long as they served their Aryan masters. It was a dark and terrible vision that cost millions of lives.

In the early days of the war, Germany seemed unbeatable. One nation after another fell to the German *blitzkrieg*, or "lightning war." The Nazis conquered Poland in just twenty-six days. Denmark, Norway, Belgium, the Netherlands, and France fell in the spring of 1940.

By the end of 1940, the Germans had occupied most of Western Europe and made alliances with Italy and Japan. The Axis, as this alliance was called, soon conquered parts of Asia, Eastern Europe, and North Africa.

In 1941, the picture changed. In June, Germany invaded the Soviet Union, now called Russia. America entered the war on December 7, when Japan attacked the United States naval base in Pearl Harbor, Hawaii. The Germans soon found themselves fighting the British and the Americans in the West, and the Soviets in the East. They also devoted men and resources to exterminating Jews and other people the Nazis saw as inferior.

Even when the war turned against Germany, this slaughter did not stop. Trains that could have carried troops and supplies to the fighting fronts were used instead to transport victims to death camps. The killing continued until the last possible moment.

After Germany surrendered on May 7, 1945, survivors began telling what they had suffered. Pictures of starving prisoners, mass graves, and gas chambers disguised as showers appeared in newspapers and movie newsreels. People all over the world were horrified.

By the end of 1940, the German army had occupied most of Western Europe, including Poland, Austria, Denmark, Norway, France, Belgium, and the Netherlands.

Instead of carrying supplies to the fighting troops, trains in Germany carried victims to the death camps.

As survivors told their stories, the horror grew. New words came into the language. Old words took on new meanings. Holocaust came to represent mass murder on a scale that had never been seen before. Genocide described the systematic killing of specific racial or ethnic groups.

These words are reminders of a grim truth—human beings can do terrible things to one another. This is why knowing about the Holocaust is so important. Knowledge is the best defense against the hatred that produced the Nazi racial state and caused the death of innocent millions.

1

A People Dispossessed

On January 30, 1933, Adolf Hitler was named Chancellor of Germany. That evening, brown-uniformed Stormtroopers paraded through the streets of Berlin while onlookers cheered.

The Jews of Germany did not join the celebration. Since the early 1920s, they had heard Hitler's message of anti-Semitism, or hatred of Jews. They could only wonder what would happen to them now that he was chief of state.

Leslie Frankel was ten years old at the time. "I had been skating that day," he later recalled. "When I got home . . . we heard that Hitler had become Chancellor. Everybody shook. As kids of ten we shook."[1]

Hitler became Chancellor of Germany on January 30, 1933.
The Jews of Germany feared Hitler's message of hatred.

The Jews of Europe

Jews had lived in Europe for hundreds of years before Hitler came to power. They had faced discrimination, hatred, and violence. Some countries would not allow Jews to own land or enter certain professions. *Pogroms*, or organized massacres, terrorized entire Jewish communities.

Not even this hard life had prepared European Jews for the horror of the Nazi years. Between the beginning of World War II in 1939, and the fall of the Third Reich, the Nazi empire, in 1945, up to 6 million Jews perished. Some were deliberately starved and some were worked to death in slave labor camps. Others were gunned down by execution squads, or gassed in chambers that looked like harmless shower rooms.

This was the Holocaust—the mass destruction of European Jews. After World War II, a stunned world asked itself how such a thing could have happened.

The Puzzle of Jewishness

The story of the Holocaust begins with the story of the Jewish people. The first Jews came from the Middle East, nearly five thousand years ago.

Throughout their long history, Jews have been something of a puzzle to the rest of the

Some of the up to 6 million Jews who perished at the hands of the Nazis were killed by execution squads.

world. Jews can be religious or non-religious. They can be citizens of any country, members of any racial group. There are black Jews, Asian Jews, and white Jews.

According to their history, Jews are descendants of Abraham, the leader of a small tribe of wandering shepherds. Abraham set his people apart with an unusual belief. Other tribes worshipped groups of gods. Abraham acknowledged only one: an all-powerful god of justice and mercy, who created the world and loved humankind.

Over long centuries, this belief became the foundation for a rich religious heritage. It produced a moral code that prized justice, mercy, and righteousness. It also produced a way of life that other people did not always understand. Jews were different. To some people, that meant they were dangerous.

Anti-Semitism and Racism

After the Roman Empire destroyed the temple at Jerusalem in 70 A.D., Jews began moving into Europe. They soon ran afoul of the growing Christian religion.

Jews who refused to accept Christianity sometimes paid with their lives. They were tortured, hanged, beaten to death, even burned alive. This persecution was religious rather than racial. Christians gladly accepted those Jews who did change religions.

This was not the case with the Nazis. They considered the Jewish people a race rather than a religious or cultural group. Jews might change their religion. They might speak, act, and even think, as Germans. That did not matter. They could not change their race. In the eyes of the Nazis, Jewishness was inborn and therefore unchangeable. It was also evil.

Adolf Hitler turned this racist anti-Semitism into an excuse for genocide, the

Jews were often tortured and humiliated in public. These men are being forced to race against each other while riding on the backs of their fellow Jews.

systematic killing of an entire people. From the beginning of his public career, Hitler made no secret of his hatred for Jews. In his book *Mein Kampf (My Struggle)*, he wrote, "I believe that I am acting in accordance with the will of the Almighty Creator: *by defending myself against the Jew, I am fighting for the work of the Lord.*"[2]

Excluding Jews From German Society

One of Hitler's first acts as Chancellor was to call for a nationwide boycott of Jewish businesses. On the morning of April 1, 1933, gangs of Nazis painted crude slogans and yellow stars of David on Jewish-owned shops. In some places, Stormtroopers patrolled the sidewalks, warning people away from "Jew shops."

The boycott lasted only one day. Still, it served notice that Jewish life in Germany was about to change. The time of the Aryan race, as Hitler called Northern Europeans, was at hand.

Jews like Edwin Landau got the message loud and clear. Landau was a patriotic German and decorated veteran of World War I. On boycott day, he put on his war medals and went downtown. He saw old war buddies on the street. They turned away.

Landau recorded how that made him feel.

In his book *Mein Kampf*, shown here, Hitler wrote about his hatred for Jews. He claimed that he was following the will of God.

This land and this people that until now I had loved . . . had suddenly become my enemy. So I was not a German anymore, or I was no longer supposed to be one. . . . I was ashamed that I had once belonged to this people. I was ashamed about the trust that I had given to so many.[3]

Just one week after the boycott, on April 7, Jewish government workers lost their jobs.

Two members of the **SA** block the entrance to a Jewish-owned shop during the April 1, 1933, boycott.

Only those of Aryan blood could work in the civil service.

A wave of anti-Jewish measures followed this announcement. Some were national and some were local. Some were unofficial. All were aimed at separating Jews from other Germans.

In the city of Frankfurt, for example, Jewish teachers were banned from their classrooms. Jewish actors and musicians were forbidden to perform on stage.

The Nuremberg Laws

Until 1935, the status of Jews in Germany was not clear. A patchwork of regulations applied in some places and not in others. On September 15, 1935, the Nazis met at Nuremberg to develop a national policy on Jews. These Nuremberg Laws stripped Jews of their German citizenship. They also set standards for identifying Jews.

Anyone who had three Jewish grandparents was considered fully Jewish. Even one Jewish grandparent made the individual a *Mischling*, or part-Jew. This was true regardless of the person's religion. It was not religion that mattered to the Nazis. It was race.

Some Jews fled Germany after the Nuremberg Laws. Some went to Western European countries like the Netherlands,

Herschel Grynszpan killed a German at the German embassy in Paris out of anger over his parents' deportation. The Nazis used this as an excuse for anti-Jewish violence all over Germany.

France, and England. Others went to Palestine. Still other Jews went farther away, to North and South America and even to Australia.

Those who stayed could only hope that things would get better. That hope was shattered by an event in Paris.

The Night of Broken Glass

On November 7, 1938, a Jewish student named Herschel Grynszpan walked into the

When the attack on the Jews ended on the morning of November 10, 1938, there was shattered glass everywhere. The night became known as Kristallnacht, the Night of Broken Glass.

German embassy in Paris and shot the first German who spoke to him. Grynszpan had just learned that his parents, who were Polish citizens, had been thrown out of Germany. They were trapped in a bleak refugee camp on the German-Polish border.

Herschel Grynszpan's act triggered anti-Jewish violence all over Germany. It began on the night of November 9. Squads of Brownshirts tore through Jewish neighbor-hoods, destroying homes, businesses, and synagogues. They grabbed Jews off the streets and beat or killed them.

The attack ended on the morning of November 10. So much broken glass littered the streets that the Nazis called the night of violence *Kristallnacht*, the Night of Broken Glass.

Figures vary on the damage. According to one historian, two hundred synagogues and seven thousand Jewish businesses were destroyed. Nearly two hundred Jews were murdered. About thirty-five thousand Jewish men were arrested and taken to concentra-tion camps.[4]

The Nazis claimed that Kristallnacht was an uprising by ordinary Germans. Actually, it was carefully planned. The government ordered squads of Brownshirts into the streets. Their job was to destroy and terror-ize. The Gestapo, or secret police, received orders not to stop the violence. Instead, they were to sweep through the burning neighborhoods, arresting Jews.

After Kristallnacht

Kristallnacht was a turning point. The Nazis stepped up their efforts to "Aryanize" the German economy. Jews had been losing their property since Hitler came to power. Now, taking it from them became an official policy.

On November 12, the government levied a fine of one billion *reichmarks* on the German Jewish community. This was punishment for the act of one troubled teenager. In addition to this, Jewish victims of Kristallnacht had to pay for the damage out of their own pockets. They could not collect insurance to cover their losses.

Most of the Jews who were taken to concentration camps after Kristallnacht were released in time. They returned to destroyed lives. With their property gone and hatred surrounding them, many more Jews fled the country. Altogether, about two hundred eighty-two thousand—more than half the Jews in Germany—left between 1933 and 1940.

They went anywhere they could find a haven. For some, that haven would be temporary. Jews who went to such countries as

France, Belgium, and the Netherlands would face new dangers when most of Western Europe fell under German control during World War II.

Many Jews were not able to get out of Germany at all. Either they lacked the money, or could not find a country that would admit them. About two-thirds of these people would not survive the war.

The "Phony War"

Less than a year after Kristallnacht, on September 1, 1939, Nazi troops invaded western Poland. Hitler knew that Britain and France had promised to help Poland in case of attack. He chose to ignore this.

He did not believe the western democracies had the stomach for war. In 1938, Britain and France had done nothing to stop Germany from annexing Austria and taking over Czechoslovakia. Hitler doubted they would take action on Poland. "The English will leave the Poles in the lurch as they did the Czechs," he said.[5]

This time, he was wrong. On September 3, Britain and France declared war on Germany. They did not send troops to Poland's defense, however. They tried to blockade Germany and cut off its supply lines.

This was not enough to stop the Nazis.

German troops marched through Warsaw when the Nazis attacked Poland on September 1, 1939.

Hitler made a pact with Soviet dictator Josef Stalin, shown here. Stalin agreed not to attack Germany, and Hitler agreed to allow the Soviets to control eastern Poland.

Germany conquered western Poland in just twenty-six days. Hitler did not send troops into the eastern part of the country. He had made a secret pact with Soviet dictator Josef Stalin. In return for Stalin's pledge not to attack Germany, Hitler had promised to leave eastern Poland to the Soviets.

Even when Hitler and Stalin carved up Poland between them, Britain and France did not mount a full-scale assault. For this reason, the first months of World War II have often been called the "phony war."

It did not become a "real" war until Germany threatened Western Europe in the spring of 1940. By that time, it was too late for Poland—and for the 3 million Jews who lived there.

The Nazis established ghettos in cities and towns and forced the Jews to live there. Shown here is the Kozienice ghetto in Poland.

The Ghettos of Eastern Europe

When the Nazis conquered Poland, they immediately began dealing with the Jewish population. The first step was to identify Jews and separate them from non-Jews. To do this, they established ghettos, special neighborhoods for Jews in the cities and towns of Poland.

The Central Office for Reich Security (RSHA), a branch of Hitler's dreaded SS, created the ghettos and later controlled them. They began by closing off a slum area in a city or town and forcing Jews to live there.

Jews were driven from their homes, many with little more than the clothes on their backs. Thousands crowded into neighborhoods meant for a few hundred. The result was chaos.

Survivor Toshia Bialer explained the confusion and fear the people faced.

> Try to picture one-third of a large city's population moving through the streets in an endless stream, pushing, wheeling, dragging all their belongings from every part of the city to one small section. . . . Thousands of people were rushing around . . . trying to find a place to stay. Everything was already filled up but still they kept coming. . . . Children wandered, lost and crying . . . their cries drowned in the tremendous hubbub of half a million uprooted people.[1]

The Struggle to Survive

The ghettos were only a temporary solution to the so-called Jewish problem. In ghettos, Jews could be controlled and used as slave labor. Many would die. From the beginning, a high death rate was part of the Nazi plan.

Jews were crowded into filthy, lice-infested apartments. For lack of firewood, they froze to death in the brutal Polish winters. Epidemic diseases such as typhus and tuberculosis claimed thousands of lives. Slow starvation claimed even more. In one six-month period, five thousand Jews died of starvation in the Lodz ghetto alone.[2]

On May 13, 1941, teenager Dawid Sierakowiak of Lodz wrote about one of those deaths in his diary. He wrote,

Jews had to chop up furniture to use for firewood. There still was not enough wood, though, and many prisoners froze to death.

> A student from the same grade as ours died from hunger and exhaustion yesterday. As a result of his terrible appearance, he was allowed to eat as much soup in school as he wanted, but it didn't help him much; he's the third victim in the class.[3]

Food was never far from anyone's mind. People thought about it and dreamed about it. They worked long hours to earn ration coupons. These allowed them to buy a few crusts of bread and perhaps some watery soup.

The Nazis used food as a weapon. They deliberately kept Jewish rations at starvation levels. A moderately active adult male needs about 2,600 calories, or units of food energy, per day. Jews in the ghetto received only 184.[4]

Many Jews who survived the ghettos owed their lives to smugglers. In the Warsaw ghetto, smuggling was practically an industry. A historian explains that food was brought into the ghetto "[through] openings made in the wall, over the wall, by channels under the wall, or through hidden passages between the houses. . . . in one instance a

The prisoners were forced to work long hours to earn ration coupons such as this for food. The rations were intentionally kept at starvation levels.

stream of milk flowed through a pipe leading from the Polish side into a pitcher placed in a house within the ghetto."[5]

Some of Warsaw's smugglers were small children. Desperate parents sent them to beg or buy food outside the ghetto. Smuggling was less dangerous for children than for adults. They could crawl through tiny spaces and slip unnoticed past Nazi patrols. On the Polish side of the wall, they were less likely to be reported. Even anti-Semitic Poles often could not bear to hand over a starving child to the Germans.

Ghetto Government

Ordinary Jews rarely dealt directly with Nazis. Each ghetto had a *Judenrat*, or Jewish Council, and a Jewish police force. The councils were responsible for the day-to-day operation of the ghetto. The police enforced both ghetto laws and Nazi regulations.

Jewish officials had no real power. They simply did what the Nazis told them to do. Often, this meant harming their own people. They had to cut food rations, force people to work under terrible conditions, stop any signs of rebellion, and punish lawbreakers. In time, they were ordered to deliver thousands of Jews for resettlement in some unnamed and far away place.

Many Jews, such as the ones shown here, found ways to smuggle food into the ghettos.

The Nazis said the Jewish deportees were going to work camps where they would be employed on farms or in modern factories. They would have reasonable working hours, comfortable quarters, and decent food. The Jewish leaders did not believe them. Something awful was happening. Of that, they had no doubt. Most of the Jews who boarded the deportation trains would never be seen or heard from again.

In Warsaw, ghetto leader Adam Czerniakow was ordered to give the Nazis six thousand Jews a day for the trains. "They demand for

The Judenrat, or Jewish Council, had no real power. They were forced to do as the Nazis dictated. This is the Judenrat of the Kielce ghetto of Poland.

Ghetto leader Adam Czerniakow, shown here, committed suicide rather than hand Jews over to the Nazis.

me to kill the children of my nation with my own hands," Czerniakow wrote in his diary on July 23, 1942.[6] He committed suicide rather than comply.

The deportations went on without him. Over a seven-week period, 265,000 Jews were deported from the Warsaw ghetto. They were taken to the Treblinka death camp and killed. Martin Gilbert called this action "the largest slaughter of a single community, Jewish or non-Jewish, in the Second World War."[7]

Devil's Choices

Short of suicide, there were only two choices for leaders faced with resettlement orders. They could go along in the hope of saving at least some Jews, or they could refuse and take the consequences. There were arguments on both sides.

The issue was not a new one. In a long history of persecution, Jewish leaders had faced these "devil's choices" before. In the Middle Ages, the Jewish philosopher Maimonides wrote: "If [enemies] should tell [the Jews], 'Give us one [Jew] and we shall kill him, otherwise we shall kill all of you,' they should all be killed and not a single Jewish soul should be delivered."[8]

In the Lodz ghetto, Jewish leader Chaim Rumkowski gave a very different answer.

Chaim Rumkowski, the Jewish leader of the Lodz ghetto, was known for cooperating with the Nazis. He mistakenly believed he could save more Jewish lives if he obeyed the Nazi demands.

Rumkowski was known for cooperating with the Nazis. He believed this was the only way to save Jewish lives.

In the early autumn of 1942, that belief was put to a terrible test. Rumkowski received an order for the resettlement of twenty thousand Jews. The Nazis wanted the sick, the elderly, and the unemployed. And they wanted the children.

They expected Rumkowski to deliver all children under the age of ten. On September 4, 1942, Rumkowski stood before a noisy crowd in the ghetto square and asked for cooperation: "Fathers and mothers," he said, "give me your children! . . . I must perform this difficult and bloody operation because . . . . [my] duty is to preserve the Jews who remain. . . . The part that can be saved is much larger than the part that must be given away."[9]

Of the 160,000 Jews closed into the Lodz ghetto on May 1, 1940, only 10,000 survived the war. Chaim Rumkowski himself was in the last transport from Lodz. He perished in the Birkenau death camp.

The Jewish Police

Ghetto leaders like Chaim Rumkowski and Adam Czerniakow were usually middle-aged or older. Most of them had been leaders in the prewar Jewish community. This was not the case with Jewish police. They were younger and not as closely tied to Jewish religion and culture. Many thought of themselves as Poles first and Jews second, if at all.

They were "young men . . . dressed in military-style long coats, leather belts, peaked hats, and high boots."[10] Unlike council members, who were forced to serve, most policemen were volunteers.

Some used their position to bully fellow Jews. Others were simply trying to survive. As policemen they got decent food and better living quarters. They thought they had a better chance to protect themselves and their families. They were wrong. When their work was done, the Jewish police were deported like everyone else.

A Policeman's Tragedy

During the Warsaw deportations, smaller ghettos in the surrounding area were also liquidated. In the town of Otwock, near Warsaw, the Jewish police were ordered to assemble the entire Jewish population in the town square. Everyone knew that many would never return to their homes. A train waited to receive deportees.

As the roundup began, Jewish policeman Calel Perechodnik ran home to his wife and

The Jewish police were young men who were not closely tied to Jewish culture. Most of the policemen were volunteers.

child. In his journal, he recorded what happened:

> My wife is beside herself . . . and is dressing our child. . . . She wants to hide in the cellar. I am overwhelmed by a terrible fear. . . . [If] they were to find my wife in the cellar . . . they would not consider that she was the wife of a policeman, and they would kill her, the baby, and others who had already hidden in the cellar.[11]

Perechodnik convinced his wife to come with him to the meeting place. The head of the Jewish police had promised him that the families of policemen would be safe. They

Jews were marched to waiting trains for deportation. They knew that death likely awaited them.

would be counted in the census and sent home.

When the Perechodniks arrived at the square, they learned to their horror that the police chief was wrong. Like many policemen that day, Calel Perechodnik watched helplessly while his wife and daughter were loaded into a cattle car and taken away.

Such personal tragedies occurred in ghettos throughout Eastern Europe. Tens of thousands died, and still the Nazis were not satisfied. Death in the ghetto came too slowly. When German troops invaded the Soviet Union on June 22, 1941, the SS followed them. They had developed a new and faster way to kill Jews, and they were eager to put it into operation.

France fell to the Germans in May of 1940. Hitler, center, visited Paris in June of that year.

Organizing Murder

After the fall of France in May 1940, Great Britain stood almost alone against the Nazis. The United States and the Soviet Union had not yet entered the war. British troops fought bravely, but they could not stop the German war machine by themselves. By the summer of 1941, most of Western Europe was under German control.

This was not enough for Adolf Hitler. He wanted the vast territories of the Soviet Union as *lebensraum*, or living space, for "pure-blooded" Germans. His pact with Soviet leader Josef Stalin had outlived its usefulness. Against the advice of some of his best generals, Hitler gave the order to invade.

On June 22, 1941, troops attacked across the Polish/Soviet border. Tens of thousands of

Russian Jews stood in harm's way. Many of them lived in small towns, scattered over a vast area. Herding all these people into ghettos would have been a tremendous undertaking. The Nazis decided to deal with Russian Jewry in a particularly cruel way.

Reinhard Heydrich and the Einsatzgruppen

SS *Reichführer* Heinrich Himmler appointed his second-in-command, Reinhard Heydrich, to handle the Jewish problem. Heydrich was the perfect man for the job. He was a cold and merciless killer, known to fellow SS members as "the Blond Beast." Hitler himself called Heydrich "a highly gifted but also very dangerous man."[1]

With his "gifts" and his hatred, Reinhard Heydrich created an army of executioners. Three thousand men made up four groups of *Einsatzgruppen*, special killing units.

When the German army invaded the Soviet Union, the Einsatzgruppen followed close behind. Their job was simple: kill Jews, Gypsies, Communist officials, and anyone else who might be dangerous to the Reich.

Methods of Murder

The Einsatzgruppen had many ways of killing. In some places, Jews were beaten to

Reinhard Heydrich was Himmler's second-in-command. He created the Einsatzgruppen, special killing units.

death in the streets. In some, they were locked inside a wooden building and burned to death. Usually, they were shot.

Otto Ohlendorf, Chief of Einsatzgruppe D, described the process in his trial for war crimes. Jews were rounded up and forced to undress. Then "men, women and children were led to a place of execution which in most cases was . . . next to [an] anti-tank ditch. Then they were shot, kneeling or standing, and the corpses thrown into the ditch."[2]

The largest Einsatzgruppe massacre took place in a ravine called Babi Yar. It was outside the Ukranian capital of Kiev. For two days, September 29 and 30, 1941, the Nazis

One of the Einsatzgruppen's killing methods was to force large numbers of men, women, and children to a ditch or ravine where they were murdered.

marched Jews and other victims to the ravine and shot them. More than thirty-three thousand people were killed during that two day period. Their corpses filled the gorge almost to the top.

A Difficult Assignment

The SS soon realized that assembly-line murder took a toll on the killers. Some ended up in mental hospitals; others became alcoholics or committed suicide. Heinrich Himmler ordered Einsatzgruppe commanders to "take personal responsibility . . . that their men

Shown here is the ravine at Babi Yar, the site of the largest Einsatzgruppen massacre. More than thirty-three thousand people were killed during the two day period of September 29 and 30, 1941.

who carried out executions did not suffer damage to spirit or character."[3]

He suggested "social gatherings in the evening as a way of [helping the men]. A good meal, good beverages, and music would take the men to the beautiful realm of German spirit. . . ."[4]

That "beautiful realm" failed to do the job. The men continued having problems. Himmler, who had no human sympathy for the victims, was deeply concerned about the executioners. He ordered Reinhard Heydrich to find new—and less personal—methods of killing.

The Technology of Murder

In September 1941, the SS began using trucks as mobile gas chambers. The trucks looked like ordinary transport vans. Victims believed they were going to another ghetto or perhaps a work camp. When they got inside, the Einsatzgruppen sealed the compartment and pumped the truck's exhaust gas into it.

In the vans, death was impersonal. No German soldier had to look his victim in the eye. The engine ran, the gas seeped into the compartment, and the victims died of carbon monoxide poisoning.

The most difficult task for the killers was removing bodies from the vans. Carbon monoxide poisoning was not a "tidy" way to die. People died with their limbs twisted, their faces frozen in expressions of horror. To spare the executioners this hard duty, the SS often forced prisoners to empty and clean the vans.

In one six-month period, a single Einsatzgruppe killed approximately ninety-seven thousand people in gas vans.[5] Even this was not fast enough for the SS leadership. They wanted faster-killing poison, bigger gas chambers, and more efficient ways to dispose of the bodies. By the summer of 1941, they had started the process that would turn mass murder into a wartime industry.

The "Final Solution" Begins

On January 20, 1942, high-ranking Nazis gathered in the Berlin suburb of Wannsee. They had come to discuss the "final solution to the Jewish problem." Adolf Hitler and his second-in-command, Hermann Göring, had authorized it. Heinrich Himmler and the SS stood ready to carry it out, following a plan worked out by Reinhard Heydrich.

"Europe will be cleaned up ['cleansed' of Jews] from West to East," Heydrich declared. Able-bodied Jews would be put to work on road gangs, where most would "undoubtedly be eliminated by natural causes."[6] In other

Adolf Hitler and Hermann Göring, shown here, authorized the start of the Final Solution.

words, they would be worked to death. The few who survived would be shot, gassed, or otherwise eliminated.

It was a huge operation that would involve many different parts of government. The SS would build extermination centers and organize deportations. The Transport Ministry would keep the trains, trucks, and vans moving with their human cargo. The Foreign Office would be responsible for convincing Germany's allies to hand over their Jews.

By the spring of 1942, the Final Solution was no longer a plan described in some written report. It was a frightening reality. In a diary entry for March 27, 1942, Nazi Minister of Propaganda Joseph Goebbels noted that the evacuations of Jews to death camps had begun. "A judgment is being visited upon the Jews that . . . is fully deserved by them. . . . One must not be sentimental in these matters. If we did not fight the Jews, they would destroy us."[7]

The Bureaucracy of Killing

Government policy is set by the leaders of a nation. The actual work of carrying out that policy is done by a bureaucracy. This is a system of agencies staffed by non-elected officials and employees. They do the routine work of operating government programs.

Many different individuals were involved in the bureaucracy of killing. These containers of Zyklon B, poison gas, were made by factory workers who may never have witnessed any of the deaths the gas caused.

Various private industries and organizations may also play roles.

Each agency deals with a small part of the overall operation. Therefore, individual workers may not feel responsible for what they do. The person who routes trains from ghettos to extermination camps can forget that he is sending human beings to their deaths. The factory worker who makes canisters for poison gas does not have to think about how that gas will be used. In this way, thousands of ordinary people participated in genocide.

The involvement of so many is one of the most horrifying facts about the Final Solution. Adolf Hitler and the Nazi leaders could not possibly have done all the killing by themselves. As one historian pointed out,

> The murder of millions in five years needed the [help] of tens of thousands. Public and private institutions participated directly or indirectly . . . army, police, civil service, Foreign Office, railroads, postal services, utilities, bureaucrats, corporations, bankers, lawyers, judges, physicians and scientists.[8]

The man who kept this bureaucracy of death running was Adolf Eichmann, head of the Gestapo's Jewish department. He coordinated the work of all the organizations involved in the Final Solution.

Eichmann was a typical desk criminal. He

Adolf Eichmann coordinated the many organizations involved in the Final Solution.

did not personally herd people into gas chambers, or shoot them down in the streets. He did not actively hate Jews. He just followed orders.

Holocaust survivor and famed Nazi hunter Simon Wiesenthal used a colorful image to describe Eichmann's devotion to orders. He said, "If someone had given him an order to take the telephone directory and kill all people whose names began with K . . . he would have done it."[9]

Eichmann prided himself on efficiency. He took care of every detail, so the operation would run smoothly. He did not worry about the nature of that operation.

He shuffled papers in Berlin—and in Poland, people died. Cattle cars loaded with Jews arrived at camps where gas chambers operated around the clock. The result was murder on a scale that no one had even seen before.

The Nazi concentration camps were located in many
countries of Europe. This map shows the camp locations.

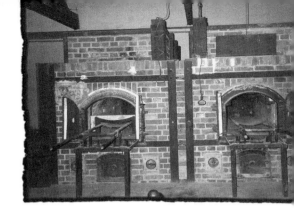

4

Living and Dying in the Camps

Long before ghettos and killing squads, the Nazis operated a vast system of concentration camps. The first of them opened shortly after Hitler came to power in 1933. The camps served a dual purpose; they isolated enemies of the Reich, and provided a captive work force for the war effort.

By the end of 1941, the extermination camps began to appear. They did not produce equipment for the war. They produced death. Their job was to kill as many "undesirable" people as they could.

The Death Factories

The first extermination camp was Chelmno in occupied Poland, which opened on December 8, 1941. It served as a testing ground for experiments in mass murder. Unlike later camps, Chelmno did not have elaborate gas chambers. It used the same gas vans that had been developed for the Einsatzgruppen. Though the process was slow, the staff worked with deadly efficiency. By March 1943, they had murdered at least one hundred forty-five thousand people.

The horrors of Chelmno were just the beginning. The Nazis were planning other camps when the assassination of Reinhard Heydrich gave them a powerful symbol for the killing operation.

On May 27, 1942, Heydrich was on the road to Prague, Czechoslovakia. While in Prague, three Czech partisans threw a bomb at his car. The wounded Heydrich staggered out of the car and fired at the assailants, then collapsed. He died a week later.

As punishment for the Heydrich assassination, more than thirteen hundred Czech "collaborators" were sentenced to death. The whole population of Lidice was exterminated as a sacrifice to Heydrich's memory. The Germans believed that the assassins had been kept safe in the city.

The Nazis could think of no better tribute to the "blond beast" than to kill Jews in his name. So began Operation Reinhard. The killing centers of Belzec, Sobibor, and Treblinka honored the fallen Heydrich.

Thousands of Jews were deported from Polish ghettos to die in these camps. According to the United States Holocaust Memorial Museum, more than 1.7 million Jews were killed as a part of Operation Reinhard.

The Operation Reinhard camps were true death factories. They were not set up to house large numbers of prisoners. They were streamlined for killing. They had reception centers that processed victims by the train-load, and extermination compounds where they were sent to die. For maximum efficiency,

More than 1.7 million Jews were killed as a part of Operation Reinhard. In most cases, the bodies were then burned in giant crematory ovens like those pictured here.

the two areas were connected by enclosed passageways called tubes.

The Historical Atlas of the Holocaust describes a typical killing operation, this one at Belzec:

> Trains of 40 to 60 freight cars at a time were [brought] into the camp. The victims were then ordered to [get out]. . . . German officers announced that the deportees had arrived at a transit camp and were to hand over all [their] valuables. . . . All were forced to undress and run through the 'tube,' which led directly into gas chambers labeled as showers. Once the chamber doors were sealed . . . carbon monoxide was funneled into the gas chamber, killing all those inside.[1]

Some prisoners were kept alive to work in the killing area. They removed the bodies after a gassing and buried them in mass graves. They were also responsible for sorting out the victims' possessions and cleaning the railway cars between shipments.

Inside Auschwitz

In addition to Chelmno and the three Operation Reinhard camps, the Nazis added extermination centers to the Majdanek and Auschwitz concentration camps. Auschwitz II, or Birkenau as it was also called, used a faster-acting poison gas known as Zyklon B.

Prisoners' belongings were taken from them as they were led to the gas chambers. After the war, soldiers found many crates of items, such as the silverware shown here.

Its huge crematorium burned hundreds of bodies a day.

Birkenau doubled as a reception center for the entire Auschwitz complex. Each new group of prisoners passed through selection immediately after arrival. A few people might be kept alive to work in slave labor camps. The rest would be sent directly to the gas chambers.

Eliezer, "Elie," Wiesel was fifteen years old when he entered Auschwitz. An older prisoner managed to warn him to give his age as eighteen. Anyone younger than that would be immediately killed. The warning saved

When prisoners arrived at the camps, they went through a selection process such as this to determine who would be killed and who would be kept alive to work.

the young man's life. In *Night*, his first book about the Holocaust, Wiesel describes that selection.

> [As] the train stopped, we saw . . . that flames were gushing out of a tall chimney into the black sky. . . . There was [a horrible] odor floating in the air. Suddenly, our doors opened. Some [worker-prisoners] . . . leapt into the wagon. They held [flashlights and clubs]. They began to strike out to right and left, shouting: 'Everybody get out! Everybody out of the wagon! Quickly!' We jumped out. . . . in front of us flames. In the air that smell of burning flesh. It must have been about midnight. We had arrived—at Birkenau, reception center for Auschwitz.[2]

Men and women were separated, and then the dazed prisoners faced a selection. Wiesel and his father passed before the dreaded "Angel of Death," Dr. Josef Mengele. He was said to be the only doctor at Auschwitz who actually liked to do selections.

Mengele stood with a group of other officers. He held a conductor's baton in his hand. As the prisoners passed before him, he flicked it left or right. The new arrivals did not know that this simple gesture determined who would live and who would die.

When Wiesel's turn came, Mengele asked his age. Remembering what the prisoner had told him, Wiesel said that he was eighteen. Behind him, his fifty-year-old father claimed to be forty. Mengele sent both Wiesels to the left. They were later taken to the main camp. The men and boys on the right went directly to the gas chambers.

Selections did not end on the reception platform. They went on inside the camps as well. A common reason for holding a selection was to catch the people called *Muselmänner*. The word simply means "Moslems," but in camp slang it took on a new meaning. The Muselmänner were

The Muselmänner were victims in the last stages of starvation. The diet did not permit them to remain alive for very long.

walking skeletons in the last stages of starvation.

Sooner or later, every prisoner would become a Muselmänn.

According to one physician, "the average diet in Auschwitz permitted a prisoner to remain alive no more than three months, after which time . . . 'hunger disease' set in."[3]

Many people in this condition let go of their hold on life. For them, the end came quickly. Either they would be selected for Birkenau or they would go to bed one night and never wake up again.

For those who wanted to live, selections held special terrors. People pricked their fingers and rubbed blood on their cheeks to make them "rosy." When it was time to pass before the SS, they put a spring in their step and walked as if they hadn't a care in the world. These measures did not always work. Sometimes, survival was a matter of luck and the willingness to do something crazy. Auschwitz survivor Isabella Leitner recalled when she and two of her sisters were selected to die by the dreaded Dr. Mengele. "On this day Mengele came . . . to exercise his . . . judgment with his right thumb and his left thumb: *This is a Muselmänn. This is not—not yet.* He did this with an air of elegance. Cool and elegant. Yes, that was Mengele."[4]

Mengele finished his selection in a few

Joseph Mengele was one of the most feared of the Nazi doctors. He took part in many prisoner selections.

moments. The people he had selected to live were allowed out of the barracks. Those he had selected to die were locked inside. *Kapos*, the prisoner-supervisors, guarded the doors.

With only moments before guards came to take them away, Leitner and her sisters had no time for planning. They could only react:

> With nothing to lose but our lives, Cipi, Rachel, and I rushed to one of the two bolted doors. . . . With a power that [comes] not from the body but from the spirit, we charged forward. The skeletal guard stepped out of our way, and we crashed against the door. The bolt snapped. The door gave way. And we were outside.[5]

The sisters hid until the selection was over, then went back to their barracks as if nothing had happened.

Life on a Thread

In the camps, normal standards of right and wrong did not apply. Prisoners were punished for the smallest mistakes, or simply for the amusement of the guards. They were even punished for acts of kindness toward fellow prisoners.

Chicha Katz, a young Hungarian Jew, stopped during roll call to help a woman who had fallen. For this "crime," she was forced to stand for several hours, holding two heavy rocks high above her head. The guard told her that if she lowered her arms, she would be shot where she stood.

To survive in this nightmarish world, prisoners learned to ignore the suffering around them. Psychiatrist Viktor Frankl recalled an incident from Auschwitz:

> I spent some time in a hut for typhus patients. . . . After one of them had just died, I watched . . . the scene that followed. . . . One by one, the prisoners approached the still warm body. One grabbed the remains of a messy meal of potatoes; another decided that the corpse's wooden shoes were an improvement on his own, and exchanged them. A third man did the same with the dead man's coat . . .

When the body had been stripped of every useful article, one of the men dragged it outside. Dr. Frankl paid little attention to this process. He was sitting by a window, eating a bowl of watery soup. "I happened to look out the window. The corpse which had just been removed stared in at me with glazed eyes. Two hours before I had spoken to that man. Now I continued sipping my soup."[6]

As the prisoners became numb to dying, their captors became numb to killing. Some did it with alcohol and drugs. Some considered themselves good soldiers, doing a terrible but necessary job. They coped by separating their "camp selves" from the rest of their lives. At work, they were killers. At

The prisoners at the camps were subjected to roll calls. Dutch Jews (top) wear uniforms marked with a yellow star and the letter "N," for Netherlands, to identify them. Huge groups of prisoners (bottom) were forced to stand for long periods of time while the Nazis surveyed them.

home, they were loving parents and attentive spouses.

Simon Wiesenthal, the survivor who brought many war criminals to justice, saw this many times:

> ninety percent of [the people I hunted] were . . . solid family men and women . . . hard-working, tax-paying good citizens. . . . But when they put on the uniform, they became something else: monsters, sadists, torturers, killers, desk murderers. The minute they took off the uniform, they became model citizens again.[7]

Franz Stangl

One "model citizen" was Franz Stangl, commandant of the Treblinka extermination camp. At home, he liked to watch his children play. At Treblinka, he liked to watch other people's children being driven into the gas chambers by guards with whips and guns.

Journalist Gita Sereny once asked Stangl about the children: "Did they ever make you think of your children, of how you would feel in the position of those parents?"

"No," Stangl replied. "I can't say I ever thought that way. You see, I rarely saw them as individuals. It was always a huge mass."[8]

For Stangl and others like him, seeing victims as things rather than human beings made the killing easier. Franz Stangl personally supervised the extermination of a million

Gas chambers such as this one were used in many of the camps. Franz Stangl watched many children be sent to the gas chambers.

people and still considered himself a decent human being.

This was the way of things in the camps. They were a world unto themselves. They were like "another planet . . . that was literally a separate reality." That camp reality was "so distinct from the ordinary that *anything* that happened there simply did not count."[9]

After the war, the camps became a symbol of human evil that was difficult to explain and impossible to forget. For survivors, they were a memory that would never go away. For the world at large, they were evidence that humankind is not as civilized as many people would like to believe.

The Soviet army defeated the Nazis at Stalingrad, the
ruins of which are shown here, on February 2, 1943.
This was a major turning point in the war.

5

Marching to Nowhere

On February 2, 1943, the Soviet army defeated the Nazis at Stalingrad. For the warring nations on both sides, this was a major turning point. Hitler had spread his forces too thin. The Nazis were fighting Russia in the East and Britain and the United States in the West. They were also committing manpower and resources to the Final Solution.

These problems were not apparent at first. Germany looked unbeatable when it first invaded the USSR. Its forces hit the Soviets with "the greatest land invasion in modern warfare."[1] German troops advanced relentlessly. Soviet troops gave ground. Hitler believed he could conquer the USSR in a matter of weeks.

Weeks stretched into months and Soviet

resistance stiffened. Instead of a triumphant conquest, German troops found themselves locked in a desperate struggle for survival.

Hitler's generals wanted to throw everything into the war effort, even if that meant slowing down Jewish deportations. The Führer refused. To him, killing Jews was as important as winning the war.

The End of Operations in Poland and the Soviet Union

Not only did the killing continue, it did so at a faster pace. On July 21, 1943, Heinrich Himmler ordered all ghettos closed and their populations sent to death camps. Just nine days earlier, German forces had suffered a terrible loss at Kursk. In a long day of fierce combat, they lost hundreds of tanks and thousands of men. They began a retreat that would not end until the war itself ended in May 1945.

As the army gave ground on the battlefield, the death camps worked round the clock. The Nazis all but abandoned selections of new transports. Except for a few kept alive to do the dirty work of the killing operation, new arrivals went straight to the gas chambers. Crematory smokestacks darkened the skies with human ashes. Clouds of ashes

fell on nearby towns, and the people pre-
tended not to notice.

The Chelmno Extermination Camp was
closed in March 1943. All the Jews of the area
had been killed, except for those working in
the Lodz ghetto. In June 1944, the Nazis
reopened Chelmno long enough to kill most
of these Jews. Some Jews were shipped by
train to Auschwitz-Birkenau.

As German losses mounted, many Nazis
began to realize that they were losing the war.
They tried to hide evidence of their crimes.
At Babi Yar and other mass grave sites, they
forced prisoners to dig up the bodies and burn

**Crematories such as these were used round the clock to
dispose of human remains.**

them. When the job was done, the workers were themselves killed and cremated.

The Fate of Hungarian Jews

With the war all but lost, the Nazis set out to destroy the largest remaining Jewish community in Europe. Until 1944, Hungarian Jews had not been targets of systematic extermination.

Though Hungary was an ally of Germany, dictator Miklos Horthy simply refused to deport Jews who were Hungarian citizens. He was able to do this because the Nazis needed their alliance with him.

On April 17, 1943, Adolf Hitler met personally with the Hungarian leader to discuss the "Jewish question." He asked Horthy to allow the eight hundred thousand Jews of Hungary to be resettled. Horthy refused.

When German troops occupied Hungary in March 1944 the Nazis no longer had to work through Horthy. They could deal with the Jews in their own way and their own time.

In spite of the Nazi takeover, the Hungarian Jews did not think their lives were in danger. They believed that the war would be over in a matter of months, or even weeks. The Third Reich would be destroyed. Under the circumstances, it did not make sense for the Nazis to begin a major killing operation.

Hungarian dictator Miklos Horthy refused to deport Jews who were Hungarian citizens.

The reasoning was logical; unfortunately, the Jews did not realize that Nazi anti-Semitism had nothing to do with logic. The SS would kill as many Jews as they could for as long as they could.

They even used the Jews' own logic against them. The longer Jews believed they were safe, the easier they would be to handle. Adolf Eichmann came to Hungary to take personal charge of the deportations. While he was scheduling the death trains, he made a great show of forbidding violence against Jews. In Hungary, there were no shootings, no beatings in the street.

Elie Wiesel later remembered the early spring of 1944 as a pleasant time in his hometown of Sighet. True, the town was occupied by Germans, but they did not behave brutally. The war would soon be over and meanwhile, life went on. "The trees were in blossom," wrote Wiesel. "This [seemed to be] a year like any other, with its springtime, its betrothals, its weddings and births."[2]

During the Passover holiday, all that came to an end. Passover celebrates the ancient story of Moses leading the Jews out of slavery in Egypt. It is a time to be happy, and to rejoice.

The Jews celebrated quietly. The synagogues had been closed, so they met and prayed in homes. For the first six days of the celebration, the Nazis left them alone. On the seventh day, they arrested the leaders of the Jewish community. "From that moment, everything happened quickly," wrote Elie Wiesel. "The race toward death had begun."[3]

Between May 2 and July 9, the Germans deported 437,000 Hungarian Jews. These people went to extermination camps, where most were immediately gassed.

The Death Marches

While the SS dealt with Hungarian Jewry, the German army faced a new threat. This time,

Allied troops landed on the beaches of Normandy on June 6, 1944. The Nazis began to flee the camps in fear as the Allied troops approached.

it came from the West. On June 6, 1944, Allied troops landed on the beaches of Normandy, France, as the Soviets continued to hammer at Germany from the East.

Even the most dedicated Nazis could not ignore the truth. The Third Reich was crumbling around them. For the first time, SS leaders were afraid. They began to flee the camps as Allied troops approached. They killed as many Jews as they could, abandoned those too weak to walk, and took the rest with them. The death marches had begun.

To stay ahead of the Allies, the SS moved from camp to camp, always deeper into German-held territory. Prisoners weakened by starvation and mistreatment had to travel long distances, often on foot. Anyone who fell by the wayside would be shot, or simply left to die in the winter snow.

By mid-January 1945, Soviet troops threatened Auschwitz. The SS rounded up some sixty thousand prisoners and force-marched them toward Germany. More than fifteen thousand of these prisoners died along the way.

Elie Wiesel's father was one of the casualties. He survived the march from Auschwitz, only to die at the Buchenwald concentration camp on January 28, 1945.

By that time, American troops were

As the SS moved from camp to camp in attempts to escape the Allied troops, prisoners were forced to march long distances to unknown destinations.

already pressing toward the heart of Germany. The first Allied crossing of the Rhine River took place on March 7, 1945, by troops of the United States Army. Buchenwald was liberated on April 11. Elie Wiesel was there to meet the troops as the last survivor of his family. He was seventeen years old.

The Camp Liberations

The Americans who marched into Buchenwald saw horrors they would never

One by one, the concentration camps were liberated.
These Auschwitz prisoners greet their liberators.

forget. The smell of decaying flesh filled the compound. The dead and the dying lay scattered around the camp. Out behind the buildings the Americans found a deep pit. It was filled with the naked bodies of men, women, and children.

On April 12, Generals Dwight Eisenhower and George Patton arrived to tour the camp. General Eisenhower was supreme commander of all Allied forces in Europe. General Patton commanded the United States Third Army, liberators of Buchenwald. Both had seen death on the battlefield many times. They were not squeamish.

Patton was known as a fierce warrior. His men called him "Old Blood and Guts." He was a soldier's soldier—always ready to fight. When he saw the pit at Buchenwald, he rushed away. Moments later, some passing soldiers saw him vomiting behind one of the buildings.

Eisenhower was outraged by what he saw at Buchenwald, at all the camps. By his order, Army photographers took pictures of everything: the mass graves, the scattered bodies, the Muselmänner who clung to life by a thread. Also by his order, a thousand Germans from the nearby town of Weimar were marched through the camp. Eisenhower wanted them to see the carnage for themselves, so they would never forget.

Generals Eisenhower, right, and Patton toured the concentration camp at Buchenwald after it was liberated. They were outraged and sickened by what they saw.

The Burden of Memory

Forgetting was not a problem for the Jews who survived Nazi Germany's Final Solution. They carried memories that would torment them for the rest of their lives. "I am condemned to walk the earth for all my days with the stench of burning flesh in my nostrils," wrote Isabella Leitner.[4] Elie Wiesel looked into a mirror and saw "a corpse [gazing] back at me. The look in his eyes, as they stared into mine, has never left me."[5]

Nazi hunter Simon Wiesenthal made memory into his lifework. He tracked down escaped killers and brought them to justice. For this work, he paid a heavy price.

His friend and associate Peter Michael Lingens explained,

> Wiesenthal [has] what is usually called a photographic memory: he is a man who cannot forget. . . . he cannot . . . push aside the visions of death, or forget them like bad dreams. . . . he has an envelope full of the most terrible photographs [he could find] from those days, and he looks at them again and again. 'Because then I know what I am living for.'[6]

In the twenty-first century, the Holocaust will pass from living memory. Somewhere in the world, the last survivor, perpetrator, or witness will die. The task of memory will fall to historians and other scholars.

In classrooms all over the world, teachers

Germans from nearby towns were forced to walk through the camps to see the horrors for themselves. Eisenhower wanted to make sure they would never forget.

will explain the facts: in Europe between 1939 and 1945, Nazi Germany killed up to 6 million Jews. In the process, they proved that humankind is capable of great evil. The 6 million did not die on battlefields as casualties of war. They died in ghettos and gas chambers as casualties of hatred. Only by admitting this harsh truth can future generations hope to prevent that evil from breaking out again.

Timeline

January 30, 1933—Adolf Hitler becomes Chancellor of Germany.

April 1, 1933—Boycott of Jewish businesses throughout Germany.

September 15, 1935—Nuremberg Laws strip Jews of citizenship.

November 9–10, 1938—Kristallnacht. Widespread destruction of Jewish life and property following the November 7 assassination of a German official by a Jewish student.

September 1, 1939—Germany invades Poland; World War II begins.

September 21, 1939—Reinhard Heydrich orders Jews to be moved into ghettos.

February 8, 1940—Lodz ghetto established.

October 12, 1940—Warsaw ghetto established.

June 22, 1941—German army invades Soviet Union.

September 29–30, 1941—Massacre at Babi Yar.

December 8, 1941—Chelmno extermination camp begins operations the day after the Japanese attack on Pearl Harbor brings the United States into the war.

January 20, 1942—Reinhard Heydrich presents his plan for the "Final Solution" at the Wannsee conference.

May 27, 1942—Reinhard Heydrich assassinated; Operation Reinhard begins.

July 24, 1942—Adam Czerniakow commits suicide; deportations from Warsaw ghetto begin.

September 4, 1942—Chaim Rumkowski announces deportation of the children of Lodz.

February 2, 1943—Nazis defeated at Stalingrad.

March 1943—Chelmno extermination camp suspends operations.

July 21, 1943—Heinrich Himmler orders liquidation of ghettos in Poland and the Soviet Union.

October 2, 1943—Danes smuggle 7,200 Jews to safety in neutral Sweden.

March 19, 1944—Nazis occupy Hungary.

May 2–July 9, 1944—Hungarian Jews deported to death camps.

June 6, 1944—Allied troops invade Normandy.

April 11, 1945—American army liberates Buchenwald concentration camp.

May 7, 1945—Nazi Germany surrenders. End of World War II.

Chapter Notes

Chapter 1. A People Dispossessed

1. Quoted in Martin Gilbert, *The Holocaust: A History of the Jews of Europe During the Second World War* (New York: Holt, Rinehart and Winston, 1985), p. 31.

2. Adolf Hitler, translated by Ralph Manheim, *Mein Kampf* (Boston: Houghton-Mifflin Co., 1971), p. 65.

3. Quoted in Monika Richarz, ed., *Jewish Life in Germany: Memoirs From Three Centuries* (Bloomington, Ind.: Indiana University Press, 1991), p. 311.

4. John Weiss, *Ideology of Death: Why the Holocaust Happened in Germany* (Chicago: Ivan R. Dee, 1996), p. 332.

5. Quoted in John Toland, *Adolf Hitler* (New York: Doubleday, 1976), p. 568.

Chapter 2. The Ghettos of Eastern Europe

1. Quoted in Martin Gilbert, *The Holocaust: A History of the Jews of Europe During the Second World War* (New York: Holt, Rinehart and Winston, 1985), pp. 129–30.

2. Gilbert, p. 138.

3. Dawid Sierakowiak, Alan Adelson, ed., Kamil Turowski, trans., *The Diary of Dawid Sierakowiak: Five Notebooks from the Lodz Ghetto* (New York: Oxford University Press, 1996), p. 90.

4. Israel Gutman, *Resistance: The Warsaw Ghetto Uprising* (Boston: Houghton Mifflin, 1994), p. 86.

5. Ibid., p. 90.

6. Quoted in Gilbert, pp. 188–89.

7. Gilbert, p. 389.

8. Quoted in Isaiah Trunk, *Judenrat: The Jewish Councils in Eastern Europe Under Nazi Occupation* (Lincoln, Nebr.: University of Nebraska Press, 1996), p. 422(n).

9. Quoted in Alan Adelson, ed., Kamil Turowski, trans., *The Diary of Dawid Sierkowiak: Five Notebooks from the Lodz Ghetto* (New York: Oxford University Press, 1996), p. 216(n).

10. Calel Perechodnik, Frank Fox, ed., *Am I a Murderer? Testament of a Jewish Ghetto Policeman* (Boulder, Colo.: Westview Press, 1996), p. xi.

11. Ibid., p. 33.

Chapter 3. Organizing Murder

1. Joachim E. Fest, *The Face of the Third Reich: Portraits of the Nazi Leadership* (New York: Da Capo Press, 1999), p. 101.

2. Quoted in Lucy S. Dawidowicz, *The War Against the Jews* (New York: Holt, Rinehart and Winston, 1975), p. 170.

3. Richard Breitman, *The Architect of Genocide: Himmler and the Final Solution* (New York: Alfred A. Knopf, 1991), p. 221.

4. Ibid.

5. Ernst Klee, Willi Dressen, and Volker Riess, eds., *The Good Old Days: The Holocaust as Seen by its Perpetrators and Bystanders* (New York: Konecky & Konecky, 1991), p. 70.

6. Quoted in Alexis P. Rubin, *Scattered Among the Nations: Documents Affecting Jewish History 49 to 1975* (Northvale, N.J.: Jason Aronson Inc., 1995), p. 236.

7. P. Joseph Goebbels, Louis P. Lochner, ed., *The Goebbels Diaries* (Garden City, N.Y.: Doubleday & Co., 1948), pp. 147–148.

8. John Weiss, *Ideology of Death: Why the Holocaust Happened in Germany* (Chicago: Ivan R. Dee, 1996), p. 342.

9. Quoted in Alan Levy, *The Wiesenthal File* (Grand Rapids, Mich.: William B. Eerdmans Publishing Company, 1993), p. 100.

Chapter 4. Living and Dying in the Camps

1. United States Holocaust Memorial Museum, *Historical Atlas of the Holocaust* (New York: Macmillian Publishing, 1996), p. 85.

2. Elie Wiesel, *Night* (New York: Bantam Books, 1986), pp. 25–26.

3. Robert Jay Lifton, *The Nazi Doctors: Medical Killing and the Psychology of Genocide* (New York: Basic Books, Inc., 1986), p. 187.

4. Isabella Leitner, *Fragments of Isabella* (New York: Dell Laurel, 1983), p. 47.

5. Ibid., p. 49.

6. Viktor Frankl, *Man's Search for Meaning* (Boston: Washington Square Press, 1985), pp. 41–42.

7. Quoted in Alan Levy, *The Wiesenthal File* (Grand Rapids, Mich.: William B. Eerdmans Publishing Company, 1993), p. 325.

8. Ibid., p. 283.

9. Lifton, pp. 446–47.

Chapter 5. Marching to Nowhere

1. Michael Burleigh, *The Third Reich* (New York: Hill and Wang, 2000), p. 487.

2. Elie Wiesel, *Night* (New York: Bantam Books, 1986), p. 6.

3. Ibid., p. 8.

4. Isabella Leitner, *Fragments of Isabella* (New York: Dell Laurel, 1983), p. 102.

5. Wiesel, p. 109.

6. Peter Michael Lingens in Simon Wiesenthal, *Justice Not Vengence* (New York: Grove Weidenfeld, 1989), pp. 21–22.

Glossary

anti-Semitism—Hatred of, or discrimination against, Jews as a group.

Aryan—Nazi term for Nordic, or Northern European, peoples.

boycott—To combine together in refusing to deal with a certain group.

concentration camp—Prison camps where people thought to be enemies of the Nazis were held for prolonged periods. Marked by brutal treatment and the use of prisoners as slave laborers.

death camps—Camps established for the purpose of killing large numbers of people. Often called death factories.

Einsatzgruppen—The killing squads that followed the German army into Soviet territory. Their job was to execute Jews and other undesirables.

Final Solution—The term applied to Nazi plans to exterminate the Jewish people.

gas vans—Delivery trucks with sealed compartments, used as gas chambers. People were forced into the vans and killed with carbon monoxide gas from the engine's exhaust.

genocide—The systematic extermination, or attempted extermination, of an entire racial, ethnic, political, or religious group.

Gestapo (Geheime-Staats-Polizei)—A secret state police agency in Nazi Germany.

ghettos—Small, run-down neighborhoods where Jews were forced to live until they were deported to concentration camps or death camps.

Holocaust—Originally, an all-consuming fire. Used to describe the extermination of more than 11 million people, including 6 million Jews.

Jewish police—A group of Jewish men charged with maintaining order in the ghetto.

Judenrat—Jewish councils set up by the Nazis to deal with the day-to-day governing of ghetto affairs.

Kristallnacht—A two-day period of organized violence against Jewish communities in Germany.

master race—Nazi term for Germanic peoples who were regarded as superior to all other "races."

mischling—A Nazi term for people of mixed Jewish and Gentile origins.

muselmänn—Concentration camp term for people in the last stages of starvation. Also called "living skeletons."

Nazi party—National Socialist German Workers Party. The party of Adolf Hitler.

Nuremberg Laws—A series of laws that stripped German Jews of citizenship and civil rights. Named after the city where they were enacted.

Operation Reinhard—Nazi name for a mass killing program in "honor" of Reinhard Heydrich, who was assassinated by Czech partisans.

pogrom—An organized attack on Jewish neighborhoods, with burning, looting, and mass killing.

police state—A government in which the will of a dictatorial regime is enforced by police agencies possessing broad powers.

resettlement—Nazi term for transporting Jews from ghettos to concentration and death camps.

SD(Sicherheitsdienst des Reichsfuehrers-SS)—The security service of the SS. The SD played a major role in the Final Solution.

SS (Shutzstaffel) "protection squad"—The elite guard of the Nazi state. It administered the Final Solution and insured obedience to the dictates of the Führer.

slave labor—Jews and others forced to work for the Nazis. Thousands of them were starved and worked literally to death.

Star of David—Jewish symbol; the six-pointed star, which Jews were forced to wear on their clothing.

Third Reich—A term for the Nazi empire; based on the idea that two empires had preceded it; the first founded by the Emperor Charlemagne and the second by the "iron chancellor" Otto von Bismarck.

typhus—An infectious disease spread by lice. Many epidemics raged through the concentration camps, killing thousands of already weakened prisoners.

Zyklon B—The commercial name of the poison gas used in the gas chambers at Auschwitz-Birkenau and other killing centers.

Further Reading

Adelson, Alan, ed. *The Diary of Dawid Sierakowiak: Five Notebooks from the Lodz Ghetto*. New York: Oxford University Press, 1996.

Appleman-Jurman, Alicia. *Alicia: My Story*. New York: Bantam Books, 1990.

Ayer, Eleanor H., Helen Waterford, and Alfons Heck. *Parallel Journeys*. New York: Aladdin Paperbacks, 2000.

Boaz, Jacob. *We Are Witnesses: Five Diaries of Teenagers Who Died in the Holocaust*. New York: Henry Holt and Company, 1995.

Frank, Anne, Otto H. Frank and Miriam Pressler eds. *Anne Frank: The Diary of a Young Girl—The Definitive Edition*. New York: Doubleday, 1995.

Internet Addresses

The Einsatzgruppen
http://www.nizkor.org/hweb/orgs/german/
einsatzgruppen/esg

**Simon Wiesenthal Center: Multimedia
Learning Center**
http://motlc.wiesenthal.org/index.html

United States Holocaust Memorial Museum
http://www.ushmm.org

Index